ATTRACTING LOOKING AFTER HEDGEHOGS HANDBOOK

Peter Bassett

Astronomy Roadshow Publishing
Other books, signed copies, E-Book versions with direct internet links via…

www.astronomyroadshow.com

www.hedgehoghome.co.uk

Most of the internet links in the book can be accessed via the dedicated website.

Copyright 2014 by Peter Bassett FRAS
3rd revision June 2017

All rights reserved. No part of this book may be reproduced by any means, graphic, electronic, or mechanical without prior permission of the publisher except embodied quotations.

Most of the images are by the author. Other credits have been given wherever possible.

Dedicated to my sister Sandra who passed away at an early age. She had unusual pets such as salamanders, newts and spiders. Give priority to your partner, friends and relatives as they are all unique individuals. Jobs, careers, possessions & investments are replaceable.

*Dr Brian May; yes the one from Queen.
He has his own hedgehog sanctuary and I have my own Queen record collection.*

"These dear little creatures have such a hard life, the population desperately needs rescuing before they become yet another endangered species on our planet."

www.save-me.org.uk/amazinggrace

Attracting and Looking after Hedgehogs

Peter Bassett

A guide for all ages on Hedgehog care.

This book's aim is to share knowledge on hedgehog welfare and keep them semi-wild; not to turn wild hedgehogs into trapped pets.

Never take a hedgehog out of the wild. There may be a young family that is dependent on that member for food.

All the photography is by the author unless credited otherwise.

This is an internet linked book to

www.hedgehoghome.co.uk

if you purchase the e-book version from Amazon, the links will be directly attached.

Contents   Page

1	Introduction	5
2	Population History & Lifespan	9
3	Population; Current	12
4	Do we have one now?	15
5	General Hedgehog Behaviour	18
6	Hoglets	25
7	Senses	27
8	Foods from you and Access to your garden	30
9	Natural foods from your garden	34
10	Garden Dangers	36
11	The Predator Danger	39
12	Cats	43
13	Ideal Weight	44
14	Feeding Stations	45
15	Slug Pellets	47
16	Hibernation	51
17	Diseases & Parasites	53
18	Hedgehog House Designs	57
19	Adopting	66
20	Bedding & Nesting Materials	68
21	Monitoring	70
22	Hedgehog Hospitals	74
23	You-tube links	76
24	Links for Reference	78
25	Other books by the Author	80

Chapter 1   Introduction

Attracting and looking after Hedgehogs

Hedgehogs are not the brightest of creatures but under normal circumstances can survive quite happily. But due to the increasing encroachment by humans on the land, extra use of slug pellets due to increasing wet weather and gardens that are too secure; their population is on the decline and will become endangered if nothing is done very soon. The aim of this book is to help the population grow back to a secure level in a sustainable way.

Note the red nail varnish on Sophie's back. This is an easy method of determining which hedgehog is which if you need to.

This book is not a complete scientific account of the evolution of hedgehogs nor is it a vet's detailed reference guide. Instead it concentrates on how individuals can encourage hedgehogs into their own garden and provide a perfect habitat for them in order to increase the hedgehog population and help reverse the declining trend.

Hedgehogs are very independent creatures, they don't enjoy being penned in, but love to explore, make their own nests, find their own food and make their own friends. They rarely respond to names but do to a human voice once they associate you with easy food but will never be totally loyal. If they find other gardens with easy food or meet up with other hedgehogs, you may not see the same one for weeks, but will remember your patch and could return any time. They never bite humans, often playful and love being stroked from front to back only; stroke the other way and you will need lots of plasters to stop your hand bleeding.

These are lovely creatures that make our gardens and parks so much more interesting. They do no harm to any pets you may have and keep a garden healthier without the owner resorting to chemicals and poisons. I don't wish to encourage anyone to have a hedgehog as a pet, but rather help the hedgehog population in a more natural and sustainable way. Human activity has directly contributed to their population decline, but we are quite capable of reversing the trend if enough of us cared. Too many people lock themselves away in their homes, verbally support the natural world but then do little else. Delaying any course of action will also delay any benefits, so please act as a result of reading this book as soon as you can.

Above; our first experience at finding hedgehogs in our garden in 2004. We put them in a box for a few minutes so we could photograph them all together. Our visiting cat never harmed them and was just as fascinated as we were. This one didn't even steal their food, but was an exception as we later discovered. We let all three hedgehogs go free in the same place where they were found.

By making your garden safe and interesting for hedgehogs, your prickly visitors will increase over time and will stay for longer periods.

To us a garden is just a garden and if you have hedgehog visitors or want to attract your first it is best to ensure safety, a variety of foods, potential home, and a fun element too. In this modern world of cameras, you may be interested in recording these amazing creatures and sharing the images or clips. This book will include all these aspects.

Chapter 2 Population History & Lifespan

The Latin word for hedgehog is Erinaceous and our own British hedgehog is scientifically known as Erinaceous Europaeus; it is the same species that occurs throughout most of Europe. In Britain it is found almost everywhere except some of the Scottish Islands and tend to be scarce or completely absent from wet areas and pine forests. Uplands and mountainsides are not popular either, probably because they lack both suitable food and suitable nesting places. Hedgehogs are well established in our urban habitat and can, somewhat surprisingly, survive very well in our cities, making extremely good use of cemeteries, railway land, wasteland and both public and private gardens.

The whole hedgehog family is called Erinaceidae. They are believed to be related to shrews from the Jurassic period; around 180 million years ago. These are divided into two sub families; the hairy hedgehogs (with four sub species) and the spiny (with fifteen sub species). The earliest known fossils of hedgehogs are around 25 million years old during the Miocene period and have been found in Asia, Europe and Africa.

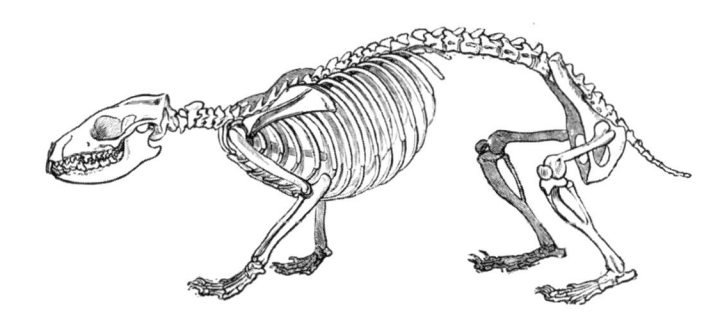

The hedgehog skeleton is relatively simple. It is very similar to a shrew. Wikimedia image.

The spines are actually evolved hairs. Each is actually a hollow tube with ridges on the outside for strength. They are re-grown constantly during his / her lifespan and old spines just drop out as our hair does. A young hedgehog may only have around 30 spines but increase to around 5000. The spines near his/ her head are normally only around 5-8mm long. Toward the widest point on the hedgehogs back, they can be up to 30mm long and very tough; each last for around 18 months before being replaced.

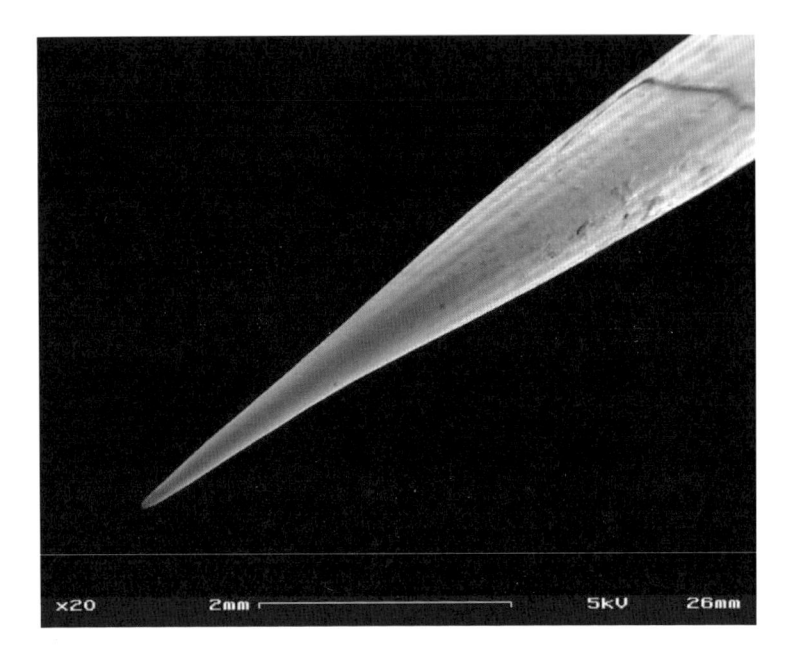

The spines are extremely sharp. They can easily pierce human skin. Image supplied by Wikimedia.

UK hedgehogs on the whole used to live in forests; many were cleared for farming and hedgerows taken away, so they slowly migrated into towns. During recent decades we have been putting down slug pellets and make our gardens secure with walled borders that a hedgehog cannot dig under. Foxes and Badgers have moved into towns too, both attack and eat hedgehogs. Little wonder they are on the decline.

Hedgehogs normally live for around two to five years in the wild, seven in gardens as they don't normally have badgers to contend with as they get older and slower, but can be extended up to ten years if well kept in a private garden.

They can lose their eyesight with age as humans often do, but the majority of their hunting is by smell (the hedgehogs that is). As long as they can't escape and get used to your garden layout, together with your feeding, they can be quite happy.

11

Chapter 3   Population; Current

Why hedgehog numbers are falling is not known for certain. However there are likely candidates and probably all are involved to a varying extent. More intensive agriculture – with larger fields and the loss of hedgerows and permanent grassland – has probably played a role. The use of pesticides too reduces the amount of prey available.

In towns and villages, smaller and tidier gardens with fencing and brick walls that prevent hedgehogs moving between gardens may have reduced suitable urban habitats. New buildings and roads carve up habitats so small populations can become isolated and more vulnerable to local extinction. This process is known as Islandisation or Fragmentisation.

Tens of thousands of hedgehogs are killed by road traffic each year; spines are little defence against 2 ton vehicles. Badgers are a natural predator of hedgehogs and actively avoid sites where badgers are present. When the habitat provides sufficient cover and good foraging opportunities, badgers and hedgehogs can coexist, but when there is no safe place to hide quickly and the food that the two species compete for are scarce, hedgehogs are in serious trouble.

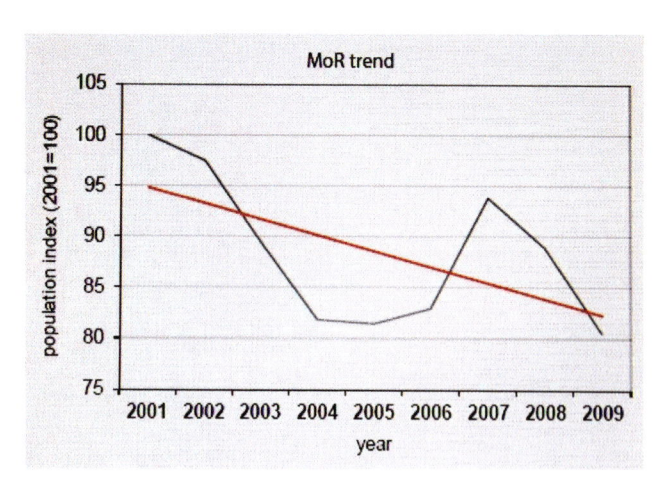

The previous graph shows a general population trend; the actual number of hedgehogs in Britain lies somewhere between 500,000 and 2,000,000. Even the upper figure means that there are approximately 32 humans in Britain per hedgehog alive today.

Traffic volume can also have an impact on population persistence than road size; as traffic volume increases a road becomes more difficult to cross and so it prevents any movement of hedgehogs. This is another form of Islandisation.

Slug pellets, regardless of 'Animal Friendly' signs on some products still poison hedgehogs, birds and many other garden visitors. There is no such thing as an animal friendly poison! I have been asked to take this comment off our website and this book but evidence from post-mortems of hedgehogs has proved the point beyond any doubt. So this comment will remain on here unless proven otherwise. And due to the extra wet weather in recent years, the use of slug pellets have increased; hedgehogs can do the same job without buying poisons.

A chart showing the number of survivors for each 1000 hedgehogs born against years of survival. These figures can improve greatly with your help.

Climate change is not helping wildlife at all. The floods of 2013 in the UK drowned thousands of hedgehogs. This is a scene I photographed in Cambridgeshire. Thousands of hedgehogs must have drowned in the Cumbrian floods of December 2015 alone, especially as they would have been in hibernation.

Longer or colder winters take their toll on wildlife too. This is the 'big freeze' incident of 2012; NASA / NOAA image.

Chapter 4 'Do we have one now?'

As these elusive creatures forage around at the dead of night, how can anyone know if a hedgehog is visiting a garden? There are several methods…

Look for their droppings. They look like thin black sausages about 5-10mm across and up to 40mm long or black pancakes around 30mm depending upon what they have eaten. The top picture include beetle shells; 100% hedgehog poo.

A study of Hedgehog Poo. If you find some then jump up and down; you have hedgehog visitors.

Produce a secure feeding station where no other likely creature can gain access. If the food vanishes, you may have a hedgehog or two. If a meat product is put out; do so in the evening to avoid contamination by flies and dispose of uneaten food the very next day.

Try placing a tray either side if the bowl of 'bait' with ink painted on it. Then place some white card or paper at both ends of the trays. Footprints will then be marked on the paper by your visitor/s.

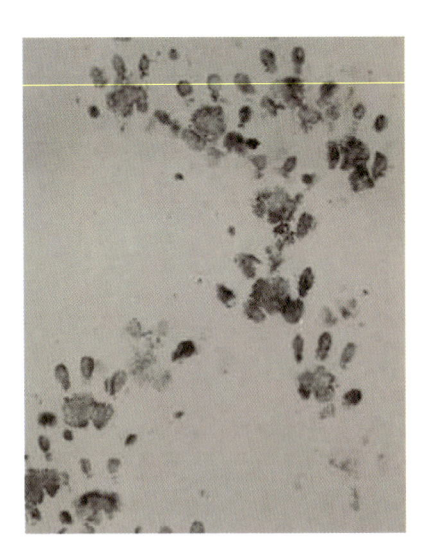

Hedgehog footprints are very distinctive. This is an accurate method of ensuring your food is not being eaten by rats.

A contribution by a wildlife expert friend; Will Hughes.

Use a motion sensor camera. Set up a still or motion camera and move it around. Set it to record on maximum sensitivity over a fairly large area. A solar powered version is now available that charges batteries during the day. These can record every night for weeks before the memory card needs downloading and clearing. E-bay generally has the best deals.

Chapter 5   General Hedgehog Behaviour

As these are primarily nocturnal creatures and often remain under cover for feeding etc, little is actually known about their natural behaviour. Hedgehogs kept as pets are off course taken away from the natural environment so nothing new can be learned by studying them from a living room in a cage.

Solitude and Pairing.
Hedgehogs generally forage for food alone. They search under bushes, shrubs and hedges for worms, beetles, slugs, millipedes etc. If they are in the process of courtship, they can 'nudge' the other toward a source of food as a token offering but rarely seen. (We have published a You-tube clip showing this form of courtship. Links are provided in the You-tube chapter). This can last until any babies are born, then the female prefers to feed herself and her young alone. The male is alone again and seems quite happy to forage for himself.

This is a rarely observed 'nudge' of encouraging a female toward food without going for the food himself. He later stood back and let the lady feed as he just watched... aaahhhhh.

18

They mostly hibernate alone too but sometimes in pairs; very rarely in threes. As with most animals they must have at least some socialising with their own species, but rarely mate for life with just one other hedgehog. Males and females will have several partners in a lifetime.

Running in Circles

Hedgehogs have often been observed to run around in circles for more than an hour at a time on grass or concrete; mostly in an anti-clockwise direction with a diameter circle of around 3 – 5 ft. For centuries this has been a complete mystery as to why they do this. After studying them for around 10 yrs, I have come to a theory that it is simply to attract affection from another hedgehog or human if they already have accepted someone as a provider. I don't think it's for food. I have put out food in their path and completely ignore it. He / she just keep running. If they get no response, the circle can get a little wider.

As of July 2013, I took in one hedgehog that started this behaviour from day one in the middle of the lawn. Once he had learned that I lived in the house, he ran right in front of the conservatory as close as he could to it. He would go round and round for about 90 minutes, rest, drink a little then start all over. If I went out and spent time giving him a little fuss and attention, he would forage for food as normal for a while but then start all over again with his marathon training. Males and females have been observed doing this.

By September, another hedgehog entered the garden from another and stayed. They paired up and even hibernated together that winter. This behaviour of running around in circles ceased within days of his new friend appearing.

Further evidence was when a hedgehog appeared in the driveway one night and went up to our garden gate. It couldn't get in as we blocked it to prevent our garden hedgehogs from going out into the road. But this hedgehog would have got close enough to smell the presence of our others. This one immediately began running circles in our driveway for over an hour before giving up and walked off sulking. Once again putting food out didn't stop this behaviour.

Regarding the anti-clockwise direction of the circle run; theories have been put forward such as poisons affecting one side of their brain, Earth's magnetic field or even its rotation; although that doesn't make sense as hedgehogs in the southern hemisphere do not run around clockwise. It just may be similar to most Humans being right handed and have no more significance than that.

Observations have been made of this circling behaviour that has been associated with a medical problem. Once they understand you are only there to help, they may run around during the day to gain your attention. Upon closer inspection, you may discover an infection or an injury that they know they can't solve themselves. These creatures may be dumb in many ways but can also be inventive to take a human counterpart of their lives into account.

I have included a you-tube clip link of this activity near the end of this book along with others. The website gives easier access. Each chapter has a page on the website with the same name for relevant clips.

Sounds
Hedgehogs rarely make sounds with their voices. They are certainly noisy eaters and can sniff loudly for food. When feeling completely relaxed with a human stroking it, they can sometimes make a similar sound to a cat purring. I guess the same happens while amongst their own kind but haven't witnessed this personally.

If a hedgehog feels severely threatened and trapped by a potential predator such as a fox, badger, or even human stranger they can let out a loud high pitched bark or yap sounding similar to a small dog. This is the only time they seem to use their voice.

Hoglets have been known to make faint squeaks and chirping sounds rather like young birds. This is almost certainly for want of food from the mother.

East African hedgehogs have been witnessed giving a little 'song' of twittering noises during courtship, but none reported amongst British hedgehogs.

Territory

Hedgehogs are not at all territorial. A male can produce a route between gardens that cross paths with several females; greedy. They do not deliberately leave scent trails via urine as cats do but do leave a scent by there own belly as they brush over the ground. Fights between males over a female are rare but do occur; it involves a lot snarling, standing ground and on occasions pushing around and bumping heads rather than actual biting. They normally keep away from each other but do like pairing up for company for short periods.

Day / Night Foraging

Normally hedgehogs are nocturnal. The vast majority of their food supply is more accessible at night than during the day. If a hedgehog is seen in daylight hours then do check for possible causes. If it looks thin and underweight do offer some food and walk away for a while. If you have thick gloves, pick it up and place it in a large cardboard box and offer food and water. If the hedgehog doesn't take it after a time, it may be advisable to hand it in to a local wildlife hospital. Something medical may be seriously wrong with the creature. If nursed back to full health, place the hedgehog back to the same spot where you first found it but at night and let it go.

Curling up

When a hedgehog feels threatened, the spines raise up on end. It will only curl into a ball if he/she feels the threat is more serious. At an extreme level, it may even let out a short 'bark.' If you need to pick up a hedgehog, first offer a little food if it's not too familiar with you. Stroke it from front to back only while giving a purring sound similar to a cat (ensure the neighbours aren't around). Then with thick leather gloves on, place a hand under the hedgehog whilst continuing with your stroking. The hedgehog will try to curl up. Once he / she feels safe with you, the curling pressure to your hand will cease and will begin to look around instead.

The method of how they curl up begin with by contracting a pair of muscles that pull the skin forward over the head and another pair pull it over their behind. Then a circular muscle running along most of the length of the body pulls together as does a string on a bag. The head is tucked against the tail and is completely secure. If the threat becomes more troublesome, then the ball posture can become tighter and the skin more taught to protrude all the 3000 or so spines pointing straight out into a near perfect sphere. No other creature in nature can perform this action so affectively. This action can be held for hours if necessary. If this occurs while in your hand (wearing thick gloves) just purr like a cat and gently stroke the animal. Within 30 seconds or so, it will learn you mean no harm and begin an experiment with you and uncurl itself stage by stage.

Self Anointing

Hedgehogs sometimes spread huge amounts of saliva over their spines. It can take the appearance of foam. They can turn their heads back on themselves as cats and dogs do lick like crazy. Don't panic; this is normal. It is believed that this is a form of pest control but still largely remains a mystery.

Fireworks

During firework displays, hold the hedgehog as mentioned above and get him / her watching them without a single flinch from your hand. They will soon learn that they are for entertainment rather than a threat. Once they are put back down, they just walk off and forage and completely ignore the fireworks from that point on.

I have even caught them just watching the display and smelling the sulphur till the display is complete or just gets bored, then walks off. Perhaps other animals should be taught the same way rather than shutting them in giving an impression that they are dangerous. A dog will continue to bark indoors as they want you shut in the same room for your safety too.

A hedgehog seen during the day can be a sign of sickness. If they are partially tamed in your garden they may have come out just to say hi to you and nothing is wrong. On rare occasions, if they feel very safe in your garden, they can begin to sunbathe when there is no wind and constant sunshine. But this one was undernourished and was desperate for food. She soon recovered after a few days.

Chapter 6   Hoglets

Baby hedgehogs are called Hoglets. A healthy female can have as many as two litters a year, up to five Hoglets at a time. They are normally born around June & September after a two month pregnancy. The second set will have to gain weight rapidly or risk being underweight for hibernation and won't survive their first winter. If they are born in October, they have very little chance of survival unless taken in and fed artificially for several weeks in a shed or similar.

They can become independent from the mother in 6 weeks. At this stage they are very vulnerable in several ways. They lose heat rapidly and are learning to find their own food. Their spines are not too numerous or tough and can fall prey to foxes. If they are seen in daylight, this is a sign of desperation; they will almost certainly require specialist help from a wildlife sanctuary. Less than half of all new born live to see their first birthday. Those that do often live for 3 - 7 years, longer if captive in a suitable garden with wooden shelter, extra food, no predators etc.

WARNING; if any hoglet is handled by a human in his / her first few days of life, the mother has been known abandon her offspring completely. So please resist the temptation and leave them be. A hedgehog's life is tough enough without further interference at such a sensitive time for them.

The mother will feed the young first with her own milk for several days without leaving them. By around the fourth day she will still go off site and feed herself to regain strength. The male rarely plays a part from this stage. He may visit and admire his part of the achievement for a few minutes but that's normally it. (I could name some humans that do the same).

The states of development are as follows…

At birth no spines, eyes and ears closed, pink skinned, blackish nose. There is a noticeable furrow down the centre of the back;

1) 2 hours old; the white spines start to push through;
2) 12 hours; some of the dark spines are just visible;
3) 24 hours; the darker spines are more visible, the white spines continue to grow throughout this time. The furrow may only be noticeable on top of the head;
4) 3 days; it may be possible to sex them;
5) 8-10 days; they can curl into a ball;
6) 12-13 days; the eyes start to open;
7) 14 days; eyes are fully open and they can begin to hear;
8) 16-17 days they should be more steady on their feet
9) 21 days or so; the front teeth start to break through.
10) 30 days; they emerge from the nest for the first time with mother to begin foraging for food.
11) 40 days; the hoglet is now a juvenile and begin foraging the food on his/ her own.

At six weeks, a hedgehog can begin foraging on his / her own.

Chapter 7   Senses

Eyesight
As hedgehogs are largely nocturnal, their eyes have evolved only allow them to see in black & white with just a hint of colour. Colour vision isn't even required for night foraging. The quality of the image they see is a very low resolution but good enough to pick out small prey. During their lifetime damage is easily acquired through small twigs entering the eye, a fox attack or similar. A completely blind hedgehog can still survive quite happily if kept in a familiar garden.

Hearing
Hedgehogs can hear extremely well and can sometimes respond to a name. During the day when sleeping, their hearing seems to partially shut down as it takes a lot of noise to awaken them.

The sensitivity allows them to even detect the noise of a walking beetle or a worm slithering around from a couple of feet away.

Touch

When young, the pads on a hedgehog's foot are extremely sensitive as the ends of our fingers are. They do toughen with age; one reason why it is important to add bedding in wooden houses that are put out for them. They don't have whiskers like a cat but the spines are incredibly sensitive for movement. Any insect that lands on them is shaken off immediately.

Smell

This is probably the most essential sense that hedgehog has. Through smell, he/she can follow scent trails, find other hedgehogs, detect their regular home and find food. A blind hedgehog can live a normal lifespan if well looked after with food being put out in the same place every night.

Hedgehogs are quite happy even living behind a tile in summer months.

Chapter 8   Foods from You & Access to your garden

Number one priority; Ensure you put out dishes of fresh rainwater or tap water. Do use heavy dishes as a hedgehog nearly always put a claw straight onto the side of the dish and tip it over then wonder why it's empty; they are not very bright. Replace the water every day to reduce contamination.

Do not put out cows milk for hedgehogs. They do like it and drink it; however the nutrition value is totally different from a hedgehog's needs and cause diarrhoea. This is potentially harmful especially to Hoglets. Goat's milk is much closer to their needs, watering it down a little would help them to digest it better too.

Hedgehogs are noisy eaters as people who have encountered these animals will testify; but what do they actually eat? Beetles are a major food item along with earthworms. Hedgehogs are basically insect eaters. However, many householders put out a saucer of meat based pet food. The hedgehog will treat this as a welcome supplement to its normal diet but will not go hungry if food is not put out. Only put out cat or dog meats that are mixed with gravy not jelly. I haven't known a hedgehog yet that likes the jelly mixed food.

Some books mention that cat or dog food shouldn't be given to hedgehogs as it doesn't contain all the nutrition they need, but it does contain most. The rest is obtained from the garden themselves.

Bread can be put out as long as it is soaked in a little water first. A little fruit bread is ok as it is moister. Chopped peanuts and dried fruit are often welcome as a part of their diet. The bag shown below is such a mix.

Listing of possible foods from you
Chopped unsalted nuts (the kind put out for birds are ideal).
Mild or medium Cheddar cheese.
Sultanas & Raisins.
Meat flavoured cat biscuits; nothing connected with fish should ever be given.
Meat flavoured cat meet with gravy.
Spikes Dinner from pet stores.
Ham (not bacon or corned beef than contain too much salt).
Biscuits.
Crackers with Peanut Butter spread.
Small fruits such as Grapes, Strawberries and melon slice.

Remove any uneaten meat each morning. Flies can plant eggs the following day and cause serious medical problems if eaten by hedgehogs the following night.

IMPORTANT; Do disinfect all the dishes regular with pet disinfectant spray.

Ensure they have access to your garden making a hole in a fence or dig a tunnel under a wall etc. Put some food nearby such as 'Spikes Dinner' obtained from pet stores. This can be smelt from long distances and a hedgehog may add your garden to its round. This action alone will increase the hedgehog population.

Hedgehogs can dig a little under fences but not tunnels. Clear a ditch as shown above then put some food nearby. You could attract a hedgehog or two on the very first night. **An archway under such fences and walls should be compulsory in all new houses.**

Hedgehogs can squeeze under very small gaps of around 10cm high. If they do come from outside, resist the temptation to trap them in; they may be feeding a young litter or have a partner. Just keep encouraging them and make life for them a little easier and more enjoyable.

IMPORTANT; Ensure there is access into your garden in several places. This is crucial to expanding hedgehog populations. This can't be emphasised enough.

Above; I lifted the wire here off the ground to allow access from the road into our garden by walking under the gate. It's a gamble as hedgehogs from the garden can then wonder into the road. So which is best? I let them decide.

By far the fasted method of attracting hedgehogs is to provide access and food. I put the biscuits under this trellis work to prevent cats from stealing it. Tent pegs keep the tunnel fixed to the ground.

Chapter 9   Natural Foods from Your Garden

A garden naturally has foods readily available for Hedgehogs. Slugs look disgusting to us, but to a Hedgehog, it's Caviar. To make it easier for hedgehogs, try putting out plates of the cheapest digestive biscuits you can find. Break a few up on a plate or plastic tray and put it out on the edge of a lawn near some bushes and watch the slugs sprint to it. The slugs can smell the biscuits from several feet away. The hedgehogs will later smell the slugs & biscuits and home-in for a feast.

A hedgehog sometimes will eat snails including the shell. This helps to keep their teeth clean. An eaten slug will leave behind bits in their mouth and can lead to infections. Eating something to crunch on naturally clean the surface of their teeth. Cat biscuits will artificially help with that process.

Try to produce or allocate a rough area of ground that can grow wild or place down cuttings on the ground in a secluded spot. Within a few days, this area will produce large numbers of beetles and worms near the surface. Hedgehogs will happily explore that patch night after night in a natural instinctive way for food or even use it as shelter. Sometimes a cosy wooden shelter is too hot for them in the summer.

At the risk of disappointing some people it is worth mentioning the fact that hedgehogs tend to 'do the rounds' and visit several gardens within an area. Several different individuals may visit a garden over many nights, which could mean that 'your hedgehog' is in fact a number of different individuals visiting at different times. The only way to tell sometimes is to put a dash of nail varnish on some spines. This is waterproof and harmless. Use different colours for each hedgehog and name them; although they rarely respond to a name.

Natural food list from an average garden

Beetles Earwigs Caterpillars Slugs Millipedes Worms Scarabs Spiders Bird Eggs Flies Mice Crane flies Ants Woodlice Centipedes Bees.

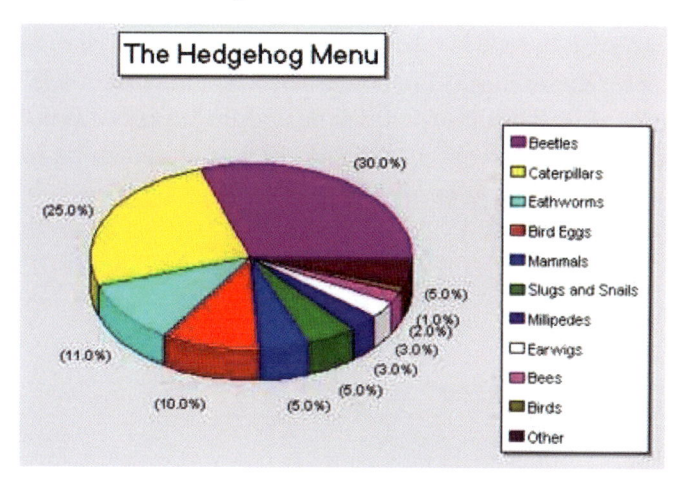

The Hedgehog Menu

- Beetles (30.0%)
- Caterpillars (25.0%)
- Earthworms (11.0%)
- Bird Eggs (10.0%)
- Mammals (5.0%)
- Slugs and Snails (5.0%)
- Millipedes (3.0%)
- Earwigs (3.0%)
- Bees (2.0%)
- Birds (1.0%)
- Other (5.0%)

Anyone using pesticides of any kind may wish to consider reducing them to zero. Chemical contamination seeps into other parts of the garden and affect the overall natural balance. We have a third acre but never use any chemicals for any purpose; we just keep it as natural as possible for plants, insects, frogs and hedgehogs. A natural balance will take affect over time. As the World Wildlife Fund has mentioned on a TV commercial recently 'Give nature a Home.'

Chapter 10 Garden Dangers

Garden Ponds / Swimming Pools can be death traps to small mammals so always ensure that there is a way out. A small wooden ladder is perfect. Ensure, if possible, a pool cover is on every night. I produce slipways may be made by half submerging bricks or rocks around the edges of ponds and pools. Alternatively a piece of chicken wire can be hung over the edge like a scrambling net which hedgehogs can climb up to freedom. Keep the pond level topped up so that hedgehogs can reach the wire. Do remember Hoglets will need a longer ramp than an adult hedgehog.

Drains need to be covered as hedgehogs are very inquisitive and can get stuck in such places and starve or drown. Such covers are very cheap but can save the life of a hedgehog.

Other Dangers include becoming entangled in tennis nets or similar causing death by starvation. Roll up the net well above ground when not in use. Keep pea & runner bean netting a foot or so off the ground; hedgehogs can pass safely underneath them and plants will grow up to the netting. Legs can also become trapped in "log roll" edging.

Containers; Hedgehogs are inquisitive and will try to eat almost anything, a trait that can lead to their undoing. Having been attracted by the remaining contents, hedgehogs have been found with their heads stuck in tins, yoghurt pots and plastic cups. Always cut the plastic rings of "carry 4 and 6 pack" holders. To prevent such unnecessary deaths, litter should be disposed of in a proper manner. Keep bags used for putting out household rubbish off the ground. This will prevent hedgehogs reaching them and tearing into the bag; they can become trapped in the rubbish or even put out for refuse collection. This could be another cause of their population decline.

Outbuildings; keep shed, greenhouse and garage doors closed at night so hedgehogs are not tempted to make a nest in them and perhaps become trapped when doors are permanently closed. Store chemicals safely off the ground.

Walls / Fences; try to provide a hole so hedgehogs can continue to pass from your garden into your neighbour's gardens without difficulty. Use environmentally safe wood preservatives on your fences, garden furniture and wooden buildings.

Dogs; keep dogs under control if you know you have hedgehogs in the garden. Also remember that whilst your dog may be hedgehog friendly, visitor's dogs may not. If in doubt keep your dog on a lead when it goes out into the garden when it is dark. They do tend to kill hedgehogs for fun; their basic instincts kick-in.

Owls; these normally remain in the country but if they are nesting nearby can and do sometimes attack young hedgehogs. There is very little that can be done about this threat. They need to survive too, this is how nature works. But animals that kill for fun such as cats and foxes in particular cause a serious destabilising effect of populations.

Chapter 11 The Predator Danger
Urban Foxes and Badgers are a major danger to Hedgehogs

The number of urban foxes and badgers are out of control due to decreasing natural habitat for them; this could be one cause of the hedgehog population decrease. The recent cull of badgers in Devon has resulted in a rapid increase in Hedgehog population. This improvement was almost immediate, proving one part of the population decline.

There are a few exceptions regarding foxes but once fully grown they are fearless and aggressive toward anything that moves. We previously thought that town hedgehogs would be safe from them and only the occasional baby or weak hedgehog was preyed upon but hasn't turned out to be true.

Do remember foxes in particular kill for sport as many cats do. Foxes may be often fed by the public but they still kill pet rabbits, guinea pigs etc for fun. It has been known that a single fox can raid a chicken pen, kill everything that moves and just walk away.

This doesn't apply to all foxes, but they have learned how to grab hold of and maim or kill hedgehogs. The fox pounces on a hedgehog which curls up on contact. The fox freezes and stays perfectly still about 2 foot away from the rear of the hedgehog. The hedgehog hearing nothing thinks it is safe and slowly uncurls. As it puts its back legs out to run, the fox springs, grabs the hedgehog's back legs with its long snout and bites and twists & throws the hedgehog up in the air. The damage has been done. Foxes are not even afraid of dogs any longer either. Instead of running away they turn, fight and can attack a dog instead.

Foxes have been seen to roll a hedgehog to a pond and push it in. He / she will have to uncurl in order to swim and then the fox bites a leg; the rest you can guess.

You may not think you have a fox problem until you monitor your garden. We used to have several visits per night. Once our fox scarers were installed, we only detect one or two attempted visits per month. Perhaps a relocation program would help solve this issue.

Hedgehogs have been blamed for a massive reduction in the bird population of a remote Scottish island; North Ronaldsay. Three were imported to clean up pests in a large greenhouse and began to breed. Some escaped into the surrounding area and did indeed raid some nests of ground nesting birds.

Reports were falsely made of 10,000 hedgehogs decimating the bird population. A figure of around 400 hedgehogs was more likely especially after just 10 years from the initial escape. Some were captured and removed to the mainland. Surveys of other islands were also seeing a drop in bird numbers that have no hedgehogs, so clearly they were not the culprit after all. A drop in sand eel populations instead was the cause.

Since then the hedgehog numbers have declined naturally probably due to the long harsh winter months.

Sonic scarers successfully deter foxes and have a range of around 20mts. On this model, the frequency can be set for foxes – no. 7. The range can be increased by using the sensitivity dial. The batteries last for around 6 weeks on full sensitive mode or up to 18 weeks on a smaller garden as the sensitivity can be set lower. From photographic proof, they do work as a fox deterrent and improve the situation.

Chapter 12   Cats

Cats are often overfed at home, but this won't stop them stealing food put out for other creatures. A cat will generally eat many foods that a hedgehog will. Once a cat has eaten close to a hedgehog home, its scent is left behind and the hedgehog may find another home as it won't feel safe. This has happened in our garden several times with photographic proof. We then had to change all the bedding, spray around with an antibacterial agent and redesign the entrance to keep out cats in future.

If you don't own a cat and want to attract and encourage wildlife, then it's best to keep it that way. This doesn't include the 275 million creatures they kill each year in Britain alone; 55 million are birds. I do realise cats are great company for some people, but they are a cause of major decline in other species. It is in their nature to kill or steal food for sport. Australia has strict laws regarding the population of cats for this very reason.

This hedgehog stood her ground as the cat tried to steal her food.

Chapter 13   Ideal Weight

Hedgehogs grow extremely fast as soon as they are born. Within six weeks they can be independent and search for their own food. The mother normally guides them to the best spots around for the first week or so. But at each stage of their lives they need to acquire an ideal weight to ensure good health for the next phase. The following table makes easy reference. Use kitchen scales for weighing. Pick them up using very thick gloves from underneath and hold your hand stiff so they don't curl up and roll off to escape. Put the scales next to the nest to avoid too much stress – for the hedgehog.

Life Stage	Ideal Weight Range
New born / first days	120-150gr
Young before hibernation	600gr minimum
Adults after winter	450-600gr
Pregnant females in summer	750gr or more
Adult males before winter	650-1500gr
Adult females before winter	600-1000gr

Overfed older hedgehogs in captivity can reach 2000gr. Purchase or build a treadmill. A safe method for gaining weight is to offer a peanut butter / digestive biscuits mix.

Chapter 14 Feeding Stations

Due to the greed of cats and foxes, it is advisable to design a simple feeding point to ensure only hedgehogs can get to your gift. This effort will also ensure that you have hedgehogs as you may not happen be wandering around at 3am.

One such idea is to use this tunnel shaped trellis work and cover it using plastic fencing with small holes. The fencing is cut to size and held in place with plastic ties. The final product is held onto the ground with tent pegs to ensure no creature can lift it up. In theory only a hedgehog can access to this easy source of food from either end. If a meat product is put out, do so in the evening to avoid contamination by flies. Always throw away uneaten meat the next day.

45

A feeding station for hedgehogs only. Well I guess rats would have access too; just put a sign up 'No Rats.'

46

Chapter 15   Slug Pellets

The chemistry of commercial poisons used in gardens or farms is complex and the formulas are often changing. Some products that are freely available should be banned from gardens completely. Generally the low cost slug pellets from thrift stores are the biggest culprits. The poison warnings on them are a good indicator alone of how dangerous they are.

Farmers use different poisons and on a larger scale. The poison has been an ingredient called Methiocarb. This was scattered in massive quantities on fields, eaten by slugs and remained poisonous to any creature that consumes the dying or dead slug. This has been banned by the EU including the UK.

There is a perfectly legitimate concern that many slug pellets are harmful to wildlife in general. Also killing slugs discriminately are taking out part of the food chain that naturally exists in an average garden for hedgehogs.

The main ingredient that represents the poison is Metaldehyde. Some are coloured blue so birds can't see them well, but if such creatures are extra hungry or curious, it won't stop them. Due to pressure from organisations such as the Hedgehog Preservation Society, the concentration of Metaldehyde has been reduced to such a level that the chemical does not build up over time due to a continuing consumption of the substance either by animal or human.

Hedgehogs do have a natural resistance to some poisons from snakes such as the Adder, but no resistance to others such as Metaldehyde, Methiocarb or anything else on the market. I suggest the best method of keeping slugs under control is to encourage a hedgehog or two into your garden by leaving that part of the food chain intact. A slug-less garden to a hedgehog is of little interest to them.

If you need additional help to keep slugs under control in your garden, try putting out cheap Porridge Oats around your plants. This can kill the slugs without harming other wildlife at all. The porridge swells in a slug's stomach and bursts if enough is eaten. Perhaps mix in a few digestive biscuits as they can smell it from a greater distance. You could use beer, but I would rather drink the beer myself; please send it to our contact address.

From the Hedgehog Preservation Society...

Recently we have received letters and calls of concern from members and carers who have seen Bio Mini Slug Pellets advertised using pictures of hedgehogs. We are worried that people may think this means the pellets cannot harm hedgehogs.

The pellets concerned made by PBI Homes & Gardens contain an ingredient called metaldehyde; we have post mortem reports of hedgehogs that have died from ingesting this chemical and believe that it does pose a threat to hedgehogs.

We explained this in our letter to the representative, enclosing copies of the aforementioned post mortem reports.

We, along with other concerned individuals and groups have written to the Advertising Standards Agency and Trading Standards voicing our fears. Letters have also been written to the stores where such promotions have been seen and in response B&Q have said…

"The 'hedgehog friendly' claim made on the product packaging does not meet B&Q standards; hence B&Q will develop an action plan with our suppliers to delete this phrase from the packaging on a rolling programme." ... 2011.

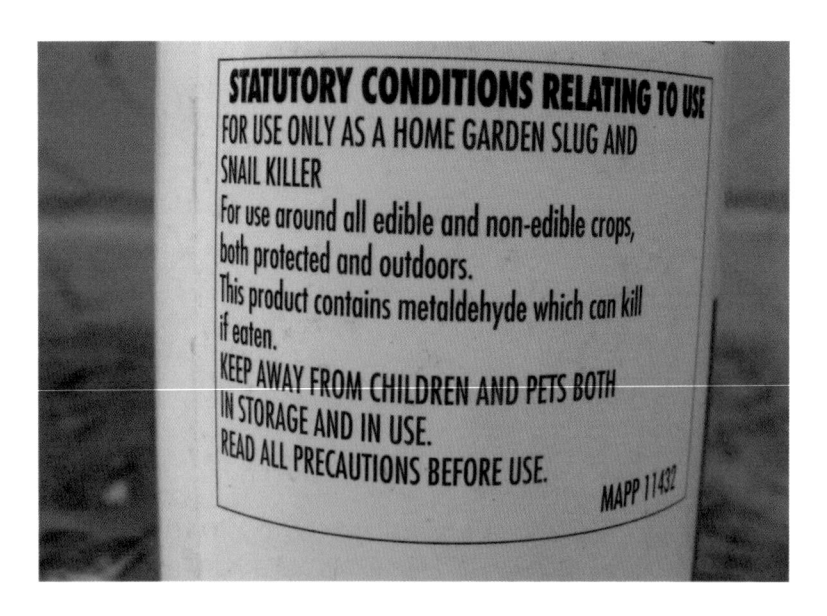

STATUTORY CONDITIONS RELATING TO USE
FOR USE ONLY AS A HOME GARDEN SLUG AND SNAIL KILLER
For use around all edible and non-edible crops, both protected and outdoors.
This product contains metaldehyde which can kill if eaten.
KEEP AWAY FROM CHILDREN AND PETS BOTH IN STORAGE AND IN USE.
READ ALL PRECAUTIONS BEFORE USE.
MAPP 11432

Since 2014, under pressure from wildlife organisations, the amount of Metaldehyde has been reduced greatly. A large quantity now has to be ingested before any ill effects are experienced by any animal; but it's still a poison that reduces a natural food for Hedgehogs.

Chapter 16 Hibernation

If you want to attract wildlife to your garden leave wild areas and avoid tidying up too much. Hedgehogs tend to hibernate between November and mid March depending upon local weather and food supplies. They can't read calendars. They may choose a stack of leaves or branches in your garden. They can be attracted to a bonfire pile if left for a few days. For this reason please build pile on the same day you intend to set fire to it. They also like to nest under things such as sheds, hedges and brushwood and they need plenty of dry leaves to build their nest if you haven't built one yourself.

Leave sleeping Hedgehogs alone. Once in hibernation, a sudden awaking can harm their health. They need security, peace & quiet. They do wake up a few times during hibernation to feed and drink a little; usually about once a week or two. So do leave out a dish of water and regularly change it. Ideally, they have a much better chance of survival if a strong house is built for them.

A hibernating hedgehog may seem dead to look at. Their breathing is incredibly shallow, sometimes they don't take a breath for some minutes, then take a few deep breaths and nothing again for minutes. Straw & bedding etc may be stuck to them. They may also feel very cold to the touch. On very cold days their temperature can drop to just above freezing; this is perfectly normal.

Each adult hedgehog needs to weigh at least 600grams (1.2lbs) before hibernation; 450 grams for a young juvenile. Any hog weighing less will not survive the winter and needs caring in a shed or garage in a pen and artificially fed in a mini climate. If an exceptionally long winter occurs such as 2012/3 (UK), then it may be advisable to consider setting up a large cardboard box in a garage or at least somewhere sheltered to give them a break. Provide a dish of water and some food that won't go bad quickly such as Spikes Dinner (from pet stores).

Chapter 17   Diseases & Parasites

External Parasites

Fleas
Hedgehogs are often renowned for having fleas. However, such fleas found on hedgehogs are actually hedgehog fleas (scientific name: Archaeopsylla erinacei) which are host specific, meaning they will not survive for long on any other species; pets or humans. Occasionally hedgehogs can become infested with fleas but usually they will only have a few resident fleas which will cause them no harm. If you leave out a heavy bowl of water about 10cm deep, a hedgehog has been known to walk around it in to reduce the flee population on themselves. Another solution is to apply pet flee powder. Just ensure it doesn't get into their eyes.

Treat the nest you may have provided the same. Destroy the bedding by burning if possible, spray pet tray disinfectant throughout and replace the bedding. A flea's lifecycle takes around five weeks, ensure the nest is thoroughly clear of any fleas or flea eggs; they can return very quickly otherwise. They won't harm hedgehogs in a serious way, but they could consider a new nest in another garden otherwise.

Mites
The only obvious difference between Fleas and Mites, is that mites just crawl around rather than jump, plus they are a little larger. The entire lifecycle of a mite takes place on the animal itself causing severe irritation. They also penetrate the skin and draw blood. In an extreme case, they can cause an infestation and the first sign is loss of spines in one region. Treatment is very simple though, just use the flea powder over the whole body of the hedgehog.

Ticks

This is another common external parasite on hedgehogs. Usually an individual will have a couple of ticks on it though occasionally there are hedgehogs with heavier burdens. Ticks are commonly attached to the underside, behind the ears or the flanks of hedgehogs but they can occur elsewhere as well.

Garden ticks are attracted by the smell of hedgehog droppings. They enter a nest and climb onto the hedgehog. The claws dig into their back and begin to draw blood. Ticks are largely harmless to hedgehogs. However, a large cluster of such parasites can cause sickness and a high degree of irritation.

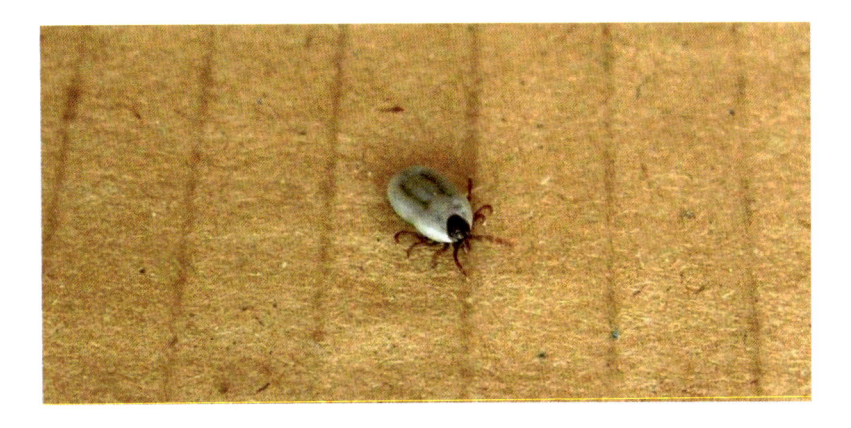

These can be removed by dropping washing up liquid or olive oil on them. They will start to suffocate and loosen their grip and fall off in time. If you feel you can remove them with a tick removal tool, then do so. If you feel there is a danger of leaving the claws embedded in the hedgehog's skin, then leave nature to take its course and just keep applying the washing up liquid / olive oil. Clean out the next box regular and replace bedding materials. If you are still concerned about its health, take the animal to a treatment centre.

Fly Larvae

Maggots / fly larvae, can be laid in open wounds ulcers or severe sores. Such an infestation is known as a Myiasis. Some maggots can produce a toxin; this can enter the bloodstream and eventually prove fatal. Such infestations should only be treated by a qualified vet or experienced animal carer. Death for the animal can be avoided if treated quickly in the correct manner. Even hours are crucial in such cases.

Internal parasites

Hedgehogs can be host to a number of different parasitic worms, with lungworm being especially common in Europe. These are often picked up by eating an infected slug. A Lungworm infection can result in a dry cough and can eventually be fatal if left untreated. A mild worm infection is to be expected in most hedgehogs but this should cause few problems to them. If you are concerned about such an infection, or Ringworm then get in touch with your local wildlife hospital. They often treat such conditions for a donation rather than a set fee. Links are provided at the end of this book to help. Start with the Hedgehog Preservation Society for your local wildlife hospital if you are unsure where it might be.

An extreme case of Lungworm will show as a loss of appetite, rapid weight loss and begin to cough and wheeze. It will show shortness of breath and constant tiredness. A vet or carer may administer an injection of Citarin-L every two days until clear of the infection.

Lung threadworm has similar symptoms as to lungworm. This can only be treated by a vet or experienced carer with a treatment called Telmin-KH. After three weeks, the hedgehog should be in the clear. Close examination of its poo by an experienced vet will determine if the problem is cured or not.

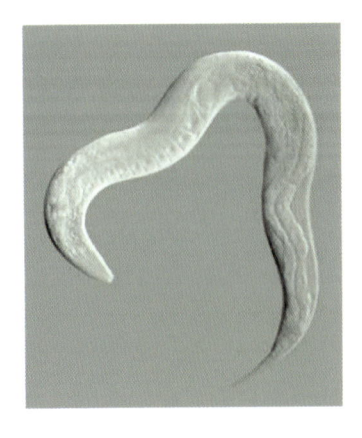

A single Ringworm under a microscope. Fossilised Ringworms show they have been around for at least 500 million years.

Ringworm can also be quite prevalent in hedgehogs, with around 25% of the European population thought to be affected. Most hedgehogs show no visible symptoms and even those with severe infections can still show little sign of skin infection and can feed normally. Dry, crusty ears are one of the most common symptoms of a ringworm infection.

There are various treatments for these internal parasites, do consult a vet or experienced animal carer.

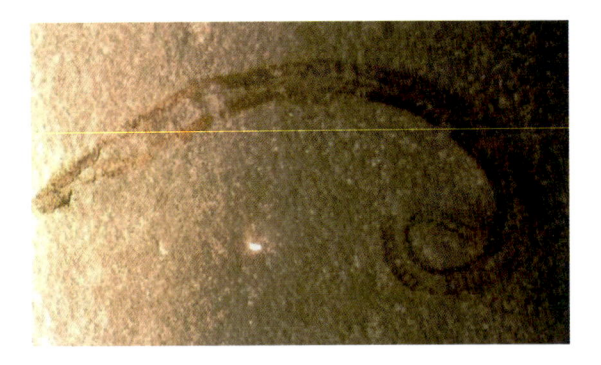

Cancer
Hedgehogs do suffer from liver cancer. This seems to be largely connected with their diet. A wide variety of foods reduces the risk.

Chapter 18   Hedgehog House Designs

A hedgehog naturally makes a nest out of leaves under a dense shrub in just a couple of hours. They sometimes just stay there for a few nights then make another and return to the first. They naturally roam around; pair with another for a few days then go back on their own. They generally detest rain and will scurry back to their home if a down pour begins. So providing a perfect waterproof home for them may get them to change their habits a little and can stay in your garden. If they feel safe and are not disturbed too much, they may even breed there. The key requirements are;

1) The house needs to be made of wood (OSB board is strong, cheep and a very good insulator); thicker the better for insulation against snow and rain. Plus thicker wood (20mm) will last longer from weathering.

2) Waterproof felt covering the whole box will make it long lasting as well as keeping out the rain. Just nail in on or better still glue it with PVA or Shed-Felt adhesive. (Ensure the nails aren't poking through the wood). Warm temperatures are needed for the glue to set.

3) A removable or hinged roof allows you to clean to the house and observe and monitor the hedgehogs.

4) An internal wall to reduce draught, light and pests from getting in such as cats. A second wall turning the back almost into a separate room is even better.

5) Put pet bedding (sawdust) on the floor. Add some straw or / and dry leaves / newspaper strips for nest material. Refresh the bedding once a week. During hibernation, leave the nest alone.

6) Place the box close to a bush or shrub or in a shaded area such as behind a shed. Somewhere they don't feel too exposed.

7) Raise the whole box up an inch or two on blocks to avoid flooding and frost bitten soil. A small tunnel inside or outside as an extension will reduce draughts further.

A design with a pitched / hinged roof; the whole box is covered with roofing felt for waterproofing and ensures the box lasts for several years.

A simple lock like this will certainly deter cats and foxes from lifting it up. They do soon learn about hinge mechanisms.

All houses need to have a 'zigzag' floor plan to reduce draught, light and cat & fox intrusion

Previous; Raise the bottom an inch or two to reduce potential flooding and ground frost problems. It can be raised a little higher than shown here. (The hedgehog underneath is made of concrete – it's not Super hedgehog).

The entrance just needs to be large enough for a hedgehog to enter. The roof needs to be removable in order to replace the bedding and your observing.

Our simplest design is the top of a water butt. We had one that began to leak, so I cut off the top 40cm or so. Inside is a thick piece of wood for the floor and a wall fixed in with a couple of brackets to stop the draught and light getting to the bedroom section. The rubber water proof lid is ideal for access so the bedding can be replaced easily.

Hedgehog houses can be placed partly underground. This will give natural insulation. Do place a piece of wood (20-25mm thick) on the bottom so they will be above the water line. Ensure it is slightly smaller than the edge of the house so draining rain water will run down the side and soak into the soil and not run into the house.

This low cost design can be found in pet stores and garden centres. Just ensure that the sides are anchored down with tent pegs to restrict access by foxes.

Once a hedgehog house is ready to be offered, do select a non-exposed position; under the edge of a large shrub or behind a shed. Cover it with a few branches or leaves so it looks more camouflaged as in the picture above. This will seem more natural to the hedgehog.

Designs such as these shown here can normally be purchased from pet stores for around £20 - £40. I normally purchase an 8x4ft 20mm OSB Board for around £15 and build my own. A two story house is planned for 2016.

Ensure the house isn't too exposed. A little camouflage will ensure a hedgehog will feel more at home, or at least place it behind a shed, somewhere shaded, quiet, with shrubs nearby for extra cover and natural source of food.

Over a period of a few years we have built up a complete hedgehog village. We have up to five hedgehogs living here at any one time and have been the birthplace of several litters. This site is fox & cat proof. Food is placed within the fenced area early evening to avoid contamination by flies during the day. A water dish is replenished daily. Our next phase is a two story house. I just need to work out an easy access for both floors to replace bedding and decontamination. They do tend to poo and wee everywhere.

Garden centres offer a variety of hedgehog homes and foods.

63

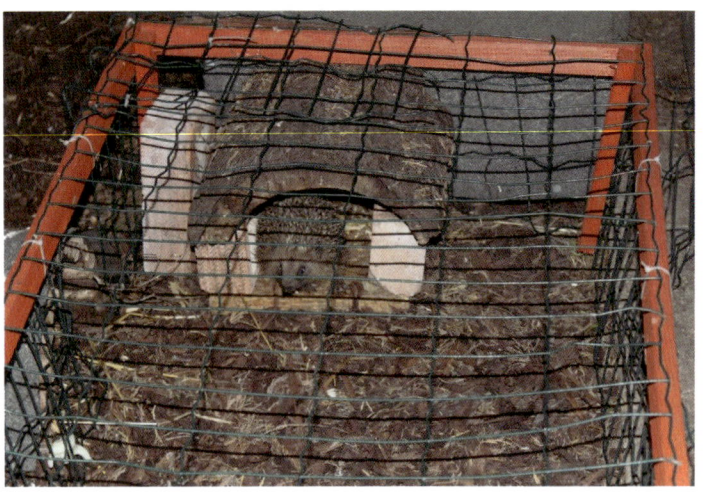

This is Sniffles feeling very safe, but free to roam around the garden and beyond.

The caged area prevents other critters from stealing food and water put out for your spiny friends.

Chapter 19   Adopting

Never be tempted to take Hedgehogs out of the wild from anywhere. You may be taking them away from a new born family where they may starve.

Wildlife Rescue centres often has Hedgehogs that were handed in looking very poorly or injured in some way. If they recover, an offering of new suitable home would be welcome. If you become a member of the Hedgehog Preservation Society (on our links page) you can become registered as a potential hedgehog keeper / carer. They will get in touch with you as a hedgehog becomes available in your area.

We also give out hedgehogs to suitable homes from Swale Wildlife Rescue… www.swalewildliferescue.org.uk)
We have to restrict this service to Kent UK. This is non-profit making. We just wish to make an improvement to the Hedgehog population, improve their lives and make our gardens more interesting. We don't want to see them made as pets, but kept semi-wild just as birds in an average garden.

Exceptions are made for the adoption of disabled hedgehogs that may be blind due to age, or have a limb missing from a badger or fox attack etc. Then a fully enclosed garden would be more suitable.

Use the links in the last page to assist. Before considering adopting a hedgehog, do prepare the garden first by referring the Garden Dangers chapter and remember they do like to forage under shrubs and bushes. The more continuous cover they have, the happier they will be. A garden full of potted plants and concrete is like an empty boring desert to a hedgehog.

Bushes and shrubs are ideal places for a hedgehog to forage for food and find shelter. A jungle – like garden is not required. Note the cat-proof feeding station. We leave fallen leaves and petals on the ground for a while to encourage a habitat for insects. Totally tidy gardens are nice to look at for humans but poor ground for nature.

Spot the hedgehog; there are three in this picture.

Chapter 20   Bedding & Nesting Materials

In the wild, a hedgehog may dig a ditch into dirt under an evergreen bush. A pile of leaves will be gathered to make a loose covering. The hedgehog buries him / herself underneath in the hope they don't get discovered by a predator during the day.

In a purpose built house as suggested on the Hedgehog House chapter, then any kind of pet sawdust should be spread on the floor. Straw and / or newspaper strips should be piled inside the house. The hedgehog will gather and mould this into a cocoon as part of its natural habit. Both the sawdust and straw should be replaced once a week or so for hygiene, but not during hibernation.

The house should be swept thoroughly and sprayed with pet disinfectant spray. This should be done in the late evening as the hedgehog would already be stirring ready for the night's hunting. Handle the hedgehog with thick leather gloves and place in a deep bowl or bucket with straw in it. Provide a little water trough to feel cared for rather than annoyed at being woken early. If they feel too threatened or disturbed, they may choose to leave your garden and nest elsewhere; they can try to dig and climb their way out of your garden if necessary. If possible, clean out the house after dark when it's vacant and avoid all disturbances. They will welcome the fresh smell & bedding as they settle back in.

Sanitiser spray available at all pet stores.
Fresh bedding and Sanitiser keeps the parasites to a minimum.

Chapter 21   Monitoring

Most wildlife activities in gardens take place at night. Birds can off course be monitored visually during the day if time is available. Various numbers of species can be counted etc. Observing nocturnal activities does take patience; you can cheat by simply purchasing a motion sensitive camera to record it all. You may feel you have no visitors but such a camera may surprise you what really does go on in your garden.

With such cameras, the guesswork as to what goes on around your garden is taken out completely. The fox in the next image may have smelt the presence of a hedgehog. After this result, I placed two sonic fox repellers around the garden. No more foxes entered the garden for months. I now perhaps detect them just a few times a year rather than every night. Don't make it easy for them.

Foxes are very powerful predators, perhaps at the top of the food chain in our gardens. They do kill for sport as cats do. Feeding them will not stop them from killing pets or wildlife.

With the modern world, new models of camera can be linked with e-mail addresses or smart phones. Every time a picture or video clip is taken it can be instantly sent on via the phone network. A Sim card slot is provided along with a wireless phone or internet link. It can be programmed to send data instantly to any smart phone in the world or to any computer.

We have recently purchased some land in Arizona partly to monitor desert wildlife. The same type of camera as shown above will be employed. They only cost around £89-£120 each on a well known auction website. An additional solar panel will extend the life of the batteries to enable images to be taken for months at a time unattended.

For latest details of this project…
www.northstaroasis.co.uk

Chapter 22   Hedgehog Hospitals

If you have found a hedgehog in daylight and it seems to be weak by stumbling around, then do consider giving some care. Use gardening or leather gloves to pick it up from underneath, take it indoors and put it in a high sided cardboard box with an old towel in the bottom for the hedgehog to hide under.

Fill a hot water bottle so that when it is wrapped in a towel there is a nice gentle heat coming through and put that in the bottom of the box with the hedgehog, ensuring it has room to get off the bottle and making sure the bottle is kept warm. Reheat the water bottle every couple of hours otherwise it will do more harm than good). Put the box somewhere quiet.

Offer meaty cat or dog food and fresh water then contact http://www.britishhedgehogs.org.uk/found-a-hedgehog.php soon as possible. Phone numbers will be forwarded on for further advice.

If nursed back to health, it may be best to release it from where it was first found. If it has a disability such as blindness or a missing limb, then a closed in garden and daily food offering may be more suitable.

Specialised Hospitals
Several wildlife hospitals exist around the UK. If a poorly hedgehog is found and you are not sure as to how to nurse him / her back to health, then its best pass the creature on to specialists.

The Hedgehog Preservation Society is a good start. Any established hedgehog care service is registered with the organisation. I have listed a few examples for the south of England. *Just Google Hedgehog Rescue for your nearest care centre.* Please don't hesitate as their health can deteriorate rapidly. But don't forget hedgehogs can feed and just look for a new home in daylight. It doesn't automatically mean the creature is ill, but can be. If the hog is nursed back to health, it's best to release the animal close to where it was originally found.

72 Chapel Street, Thatcham, Berkshire
www.hedgehog-rescue.org.uk

London Colney Hedgehog Rescue
Near St Albans AL2 1PP   Phone: 07867 567464
http://londoncolneyhedgehogrescue.weebly.com

The Broadwater Forest Wildlife Hospital
Fairview Lane, Tunbridge Wells TN3 9LU
www.follywildliferescue.org.uk

Prickles Hedgehog Rescue
Cheddar
Somerset   Tel: 07806 744 772
www.prickleshedgehogrescue.org.uk

Brian May's 'Amazing Grace' Hedgehog sanctuary.
P.O. BOX 141, Windlesham, Surrey, GU20 6YW
Email: info@gracethehedgehog.co.uk   01344 623106
www.save-me.org.uk/amazinggrace

Chapter 23   You-tube links

To add extra interest and to explain matters to in a form that a normal book cannot perform, we have included a number of clips. These are all links to you-tube and some are posted by the author of this book. They can be accessed more easily via
www.hedgehoghome.co.uk

Running in circles
This hedgehog survived poisoned slug pellets. Once in his newly adopted home, he immediately tries to attract friends via this unusual behaviour. Most of the time they run anti-clockwise, this one must be 'left handed.'

Shoo off Cat!
Hedgehogs are brave enough to scare off cats sometimes if out in the open. The reaction can vary from one situation to another. We have made our hedgehog village secure from cats as best we can. They do steal food and make the hedgehogs feel insecure if they enter their home and may even abandon the home and move elsewhere.

Noisy eating
Hedgehogs are very noisy and sometimes messy eaters with no table manners. This is Spike with no camera shyness. He signed a publicity waver form… if you believe that, you will believe the moon landings were fake.

Assisting deep steps
If you have deep steps that a hedgehog may have difficulty with, then perhaps a plank of wood will help.

Swimming Hedgehog
Hedgehogs can swim for short periods and seem to enjoy the experience. But if you have a pond, please ensure an easy escape route for them or even put up an unclimbable fence.

General advice
Great supporting video connecting some of the advice given in the book. I do think this lady is wrong about the cat food advice though from 10yrs experience. Hedgehogs definitely prefer gravy soaked food rather than jelly.

Hoglets
This is an amazing short clip of a typical litter of three Hoglets being fed by mummy.

I try not to encourage people having hedgehogs as pets, but these Hoglets are so cute…

Courtship
When a male tries to befriend a female, he often nudges the female toward food or water without taking any for himself… until she isn't looking.

Fighting
Rival males can fight over a female. They very rarely bite, but just push and shove with a lot of snorting. They do not fight over territory.

Chapter 24   Links for Reference / Further Reading

Our own website… www.hedgehoghome.co.uk

These links as well as others are found there.

http://www.swalewildliferescue.org.uk

Ingrid Cole, is the operator of the Swale Wildlife Rescue. Free advice is given, along with a hedgehog adoption in exchange for a donation to this non-profit service.

http://www.britishhedgehogs.org.uk/

The main society to help hedgehog preservation in the UK; very low subscription rate, ideal for children as well as adults.

http://www.foxolutions.co.uk

Ideas for reducing Fox visits to your garden. They sometimes attack hedgehogs for sport and not even eat them. Same goes for rabbits, guinea pigs, chickens etc.

http://hedgehoghelp.co.uk

http://www.hedgehogstreet.org

For further advice on attracting and looking after hedgehogs by other enthusiasts.

Our garden has been featured on the BBC in 2013 as an example of attracting and supporting nature. Our friend Rolf Williams from the RSPB is being interviewed.

Chapter 25   Other books by the Author

New books will be published in the coming years. Refer to www.astronomyroadshow.com for signed copies, updated listings and direct links. The following are available…

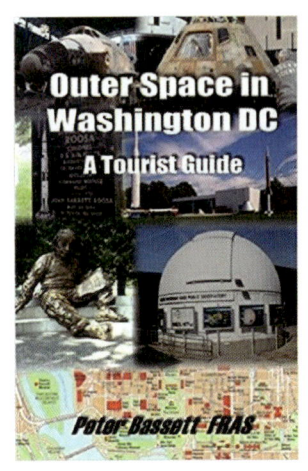

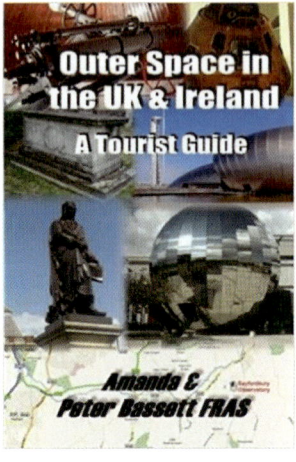

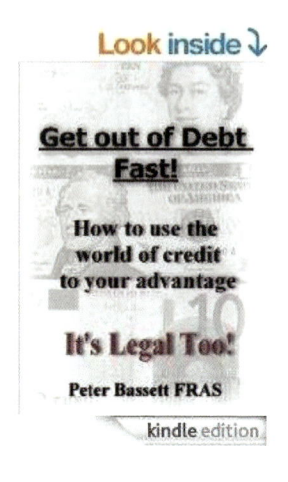

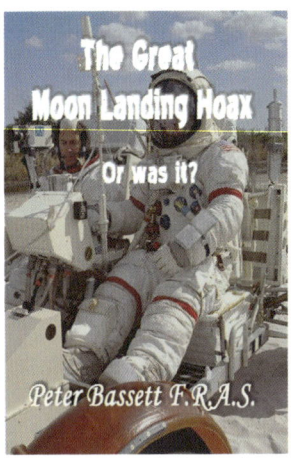

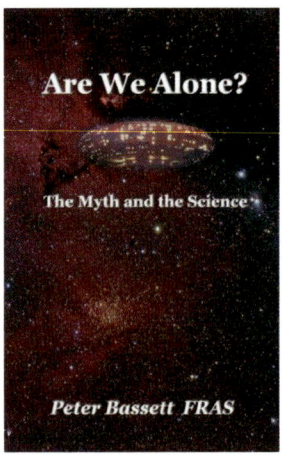

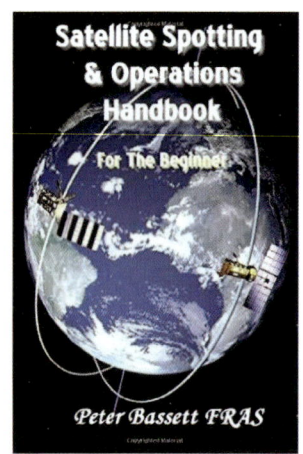

All books and various versions can be found on the books page of
www.astronomyroadshow.com

There are B&W, Colour and e-book versions. All book sales support four charities;

Cancer Research UK

Kent Air Ambulance

Smile Malawi Orphanage in Africa

British Hedgehog Preservation Society

Printed in Great Britain
by Amazon